Prairie Fisherman:
Fishing Memories

Other Works By Brian Hesje

Prairie Boomer: Farm Boy Memories
Paperback ISBN: 978-1-9994418-6-9
E-Book ISBN: 978-1-9994418-7-6

Thoughts on Thinking
Paperback ISBN: 978-1-9994418-1-4

26 Thoughts on Leadership
Paperback ISBN: 978-1-9994418-2-1

Why Save Your Golf Balls?
Paperback ISBN: 978-1-9994418-0-7

Prairie Fisherman: Fishing Memories

BRIAN W. HESJE

PRAIRIE FISHERMAN:
FISHING MEMORIES

Published by Brian Hesje, Edmonton, Canada

Paperback ISBN: 978-1-9994418-6-9
Ebook ISBN: 978-1-9994418-7-6

First Print: January 2021

Publication assistance and digital printing in Canada by

PUBLISHING
PageMasterPublishing.ca

CONTENTS

INTRODUCTION

What is your favourite hobby? Many people say they are too busy to have a hobby. I used to be one of those people. That belief changed for me one night while playing poker. Somehow the conversation turned to fishing. The most enthusiastic person was me. That is until one of the guys asked me how often I planned fishing trips. That question turned on the light. None of us have time to pursue our hobbies unless we MAKE time to do so. That night I vowed to myself another year would never pass without having at least one fishing trip. And to date, one year has not!

Just as the attitudes of people who sport fish have changed over the decades, so have mine. In the 1950's as a boy my purpose for fishing was providing food for my family. In the 1960's my teen years focused on education and improving social skills, not necessarily in that order, so I didn't make time to fish. In the 1970's I was introduced to 'barbless' hooks. The barbs gave the fish less chance of escape and were more damaging to its mouth. I began to view fishing as a sport rather than a food source. In the 1980's it became more common for me to catch and release fish.

In the 1990's I discovered that pictures and measurements,

not the actual fish, were sent to the taxidermist. Conservation was now being discussed. In the 21st century, releasing fish, particularly large fish, became much more prevalent. Conservation and even 'tagging' fish before releasing them became part of my experience. Tagging fish enables very useful data to be collected to assist in research to preserve the species.

Fishing has given me much more than I have given fishing. I spent countless hours on or near water, surrounded by fresh air and the beauty of nature. I have had hours of interesting conversation with friends and acquaintances. I have had so much laughter that tears rolled down my cheeks. I have travelled from Edmonton, Alberta to parts of the world that I would never have visited. I gained an appreciation of the importance of the environment and conservation.

I saw every tug on the line as a record catch. Maybe most of all, fishing gave me an opportunity to compete. Many people would not think of fishing as a competitive activity. My goal was to catch the record size fish or if not, the biggest fish in my group.

Growing up, I was my own guide. In my twenties and thirties, most of my fishing was self-guided, with my friends as the guides and I being the self. After turning 40, I fished almost exclusively with professional guides.

I have categorized my fishing experiences by type of water. Lake, river, and ocean fishing are vastly different experiences, requiring different types of tackle, bait, mentality, skills, and preparation. Fishing has been a lifelong learning experience for me. I have learned fishing requires patience, fishing requires luck, and for best results, fishing requires money.

Fishing can be done alone and as a boy, I fished many hours by myself. But after my teen years I seldom ever fished solo. I never lost my love of solitude by a river, but I did lose interest in fishing alone. I fished with my daughter Allison and her husband Rynhard. I fished with my wife Wynne. I fished with each of my three brothers. I fished with my good friends Craig, Keith, and Rick. I fished with my lawyer Ron, my auditor Rick, many people from work and many business associates. Some of the people I have lost touch with and some are still friends today.

RIVERS

1

SASKATCHEWAN RIVER

Goldeye

The North and South Saskatchewan Rivers meet to become the Saskatchewan River just east of Prince Albert, Saskatchewan. The mouth of the North Saskatchewan River is in the Rocky Mountains at Saskatchewan Crossing in Alberta. The South Saskatchewan River begins in Southern Alberta near Medicine Hat where the Oldman and Bow Rivers meet.

I grew up in the 1950's on a farm about fifty kilometres from Prince Albert near the town of Birch Hills. The North Saskatchewan River runs through Prince Albert and the South Saskatchewan River runs right past our farm. The two rivers meet about thirty kilometres from my home at what is known as the Saskatchewan River Forks. It eventually empties into Lake Winnipeg in Manitoba and finally into Hudson Bay.

Many visitors to our farm commented on the river's beauty as it flowed past our home. As a boy growing up there, the river meant two things. It was a good place to swim and a great place to fish. We didn't have swimming lessons on the farm so 'dog-paddling' described our swimming more accurately. I spent hours swimming but many more hours fishing.

As a beginning fisherman I had little knowledge, little money, and little skill to get started. My dad took me to Botham's Hardware in Birch Hills. I didn't need an expensive rod and reel, tackle box or lures. I only needed a green, braided fishing line, some small hooks, and some leaders, all for less than $5.

I tied a rock to the end of the line. The rock had to be large enough to anchor the line in the river, but small enough to throw. The distance of the line was about fifty feet. Starting about a yard from the rock, I tied four leaders to the line, with small bare hooks attached and spaced three feet apart. For the final step, I wrapped the line around a wooden stake.

The soil along the river was too sandy for my preferred choice of bait, earthworms, which left me with the less desirable task of catching grasshoppers. If you aren't familiar with grasshoppers, they jump long distances, making them difficult to catch. Earthworms require only a little digging, and they possess no jumping ability. But there is a strategy to effective grasshopper catching. Go after them in the morning. They can't hop as far or as fast when they are covered in dew. Many mornings I got up early to catch grasshoppers. and put them in an empty coke bottle.

It was only a ten-minute walk from home to my fishing spot on the river. where I unraveled the line and pounded a stake into the ground. Then I then cut a willow branch and stuck it in the ground six inches from the stake and slack-tied my line between the two. I then baited the four hooks with grasshoppers and threw the line in the river. I caught hundreds of goldeye using that simple method. I would sit and watch for the willow to jerk meaning a fish was on the line. I spent many hours alone with my thoughts sitting on the riverbank waiting for the fish. I didn't have to be there to catch a fish. I could go for a swim and catch a fish. I could go home for lunch and catch a fish. I didn't have to see the willow jerk, but it was exciting experiencing that magic moment.

Goldeye are silver in colour, usually under three pounds, and predictably, have goldeyes. I learned to scale and clean the fish and take them home to eat fresh or put in the deep freeze. Not once did my mom say we had too many fish and it never occurred to me we might. To my knowledge, no one in the family ever got tired of eating them.

My birthday is in September, harvest time on a farm. I think on my 10th birthday, we made a family trip to the 'forks.' The forks, where the North and South Saskatchewan Rivers meet, is known for its great fishing.

We caught some fish, but my allergies really flared up. In addition to my usual runny nose, my eyes swelled almost shut. My mother was very understanding, but not so much my brothers. I think it may have reminded them that I often fished while they stacked hay bales. Despite the allergy attack, realizing my parents made such a big sacrifice for that day still makes it one of my fondest birthdays.

Most people don't think of fishing as a competitive sport, but it always was for me. As a kid in the '50's, I submitted my largest catch to the Saskatchewan Fisheries to win the year's record sized goldeye. I never won but came close a couple of times, almost landing about a three-pounder. Today the goldeye population is so depleted in the river Saskatchewan Fisheries no longer tracks the largest fish. When I reached high school, it seemed other interests took on a greater importance than fishing. I didn't fish for goldeye for several decades.

My daughter was a young lady when I caught my last goldeye. I booked a fishing trip with 'Get Hooked' to fish for goldeye in the North Saskatchewan River. As a youth I caught all goldeye and no pickerel. Now we were catching all pickerel and no goldeye. The highlight of the trip for me was finally catching one goldeye which we released. I think the highlight for Allison was me losing my sunglasses. I was sure I had left them in the guide's truck, but he said no. Gone were the days when I fished to feed the family, it was now for sport. I tried fishing a few more times at the farm with a rod and reel, but with no luck catching goldeye.

Fishing for goldeye in the Saskatchewan River created a lifelong love of fishing for me. Interesting that even alone I could create a competition.

Brian with last goldeye ever caught

2

PUDDLE NEAR HINTON, ALBERTA

No fish

Just as fishing trips can lead to other opportunities, other opportunities can lead to fishing trips. I took one fishing trip because of curling, a popular sport in Canada, that often appears humorous to those unfamiliar with it. Curling is played on ice, with two teams. The objective is to slide a rock weighing between 38-44 pounds on a sheet of ice a hundred and fifty feet long toward a target area which is segmented into four concentric circles. A team consists of four players, a lead, a second, a third and a skip who each slide two rocks, sweep the ice ahead of its path, and discuss strategy. The team with the rocks closest to the centre of the circle or 'house' scores. I skipped our curling team with Craig, a sales manager as third, Roy, an engineer as second, and Henry, an electrician as lead. We curled twice a week for years.

We were all in our 20's and had ping pong tables at our houses. We'd play ping pong after curling, often not getting home until the wee hours of the morning. Since we had so much fun in the winter, we decided to also do so in the summer. We scheduled a fishing trip in the waters near Hinton, Alberta. Hinton is about a three-hour drive west of Edmonton near the Rocky Mountains. We got all the necessary gear, and Henry loaded his truck for the big trip.

Unfortunately, it rained a lot the days before we left. Our wives all recommended we cancel and go when the weather was better, but we were much too smart to take that advice. We set out on Friday night as a happy bunch. It was obvious during our drive that we had made a mistake, but we carried on. We set up the tent and had dinner, but the creeks were running much too fast for fishing. That night, Craig, Henry, and I got cold in the tent, so we went outside and built a fire. We were visiting and warming up when Roy poked his head out and said, "Wow, it's sure warm out here." The next morning, we packed up and headed home.

Driving back, we stopped at a campsite along the highway for lunch. The facilities are free and can accommodate more than one group. There was already a young couple there preparing their lunch. When we arrived, Roy jumped out of the truck, and started fishing in a puddle of water left by the rain. Henry stuck an axe in the campsite roof to hold a tarp as shelter from the wind. The couple must have thought we had escaped from an institution. . Whatever they thought, the result was that the husband said, "Put everything in the vehicle, we are leaving." We are still not sure if he turned off their Coleman stove before heading out. We thought it funny at the time but perhaps they did not.

We arrived back in Edmonton a day early and with no fish. I don't think we heard one, "I told you so." Had the shoe been on the other foot, it is unlikely we would have been so kind. A fishing trip with many laughs but not only no fish, no fishing.

Craig Benfield, Roy Berg, Brian Hesje, Henry Caley

3

CHRISTMAS CREEK, ALBERTA

Grayling

Christmas Creek is near the hamlet of Blue Ridge midway between the towns of Whitecourt and Mayerthorpe. It is about an hour and a half drive northwest of Edmonton. My friends Vern and Ernie, both former residents of Mayerthorpe, had fished the creek many times. I was invited to join them and their sons for a day of fishing for grayling. Grayling are small fish that rarely reach twenty inches in size.

We met at their office, and we headed out in separate SUVs, each hauling a trailer loaded with an Argo ATV. Add in the cost of fishing gear and quite a large investment had been made to go fishing. We arrived at the end of the road. The ATV's were unloaded and packed with the gear and we headed out for the creek. Once we arrived at the fishing spot my instinct was to get a line in the water immediately.

You can't catch fish without a hook in the water!

However, Vern said, "I'm a bit hungry. What say we build a small fire and roast a couple of wieners?"

Then he added, "Anyone that is in a hurry to fish doesn't know how to enjoy fishing."

Obviously, I didn't know how to fish. Making a fire, roasting a wiener, and eating a hotdog was surprisingly enjoyable. It also enabled me to appreciate the beauty of the surroundings.

We spent the next few hours fishing different holes. I don't remember catching much grayling, but I do remember the experience and lesson.

Fishing allows you to appreciate the wonders of nature and to relax. Its primary purpose should be the fishing not the catching. Everything doesn't have to be a competition.

4

ATLIN RIVER, BRITISH COLUMBIA

Salmon

In the late 1970's I went on my second fishing trip courtesy of Vern and Ernie. Instead of ATV's, this time we chartered a plane from Edmonton to Atlin, an isolated community of about 500. It is about a three-hour drive from Whitehorse, Yukon or Skagway, Alaska, and about a four-hour flight northwest of Edmonton Alberta.

Atlin's population peaked at 5,000 during the Klondike Gold Rush in 1898, as it was one of the richest rush offshoots with over 23 million dollars' worth of gold.

We didn't catch much. I don't personally recall landing a single fish.

However, I do remember our charter landed at a camp on what I believe was the shore of the Atlin River. The camp was unguided, but we had all the necessary supplies. Unfortunately, the fishing was not very good, and neither was the catching. To make matters worse the sky turned dark with smoke from a nearby forest fire. We knew you could be required to help fight the fire if there was a shortage of firefighters. Fortunately, that did not happen but what did happen is our helicopter ride out was cancelled so it could be used to help fight the fire.

A few days later, with the fire finally under control, a helicopter finally arrived to fly us out of there. While small and old, we were grateful to see it. About five minutes from landing at the airport, the passenger door fell off, crashing to the ground. Fortunately, I was not aware of the danger and found it amusing. The pilot acted like this happened all the time.

We were so glad to get out of there. I still remember feeling so happy to crawl into my bed back home in Edmonton. I would prefer to remember a fishing trip for catching a fish rather than escaping fighting a fire.

Brian, Randy, Vern, Larry, Ernie, Kevin

5

TREE RIVER, NUNAVUT, CANADA

Arctic Char

Tree River has the world record for Arctic Char caught on a rod and reel at 32 pounds, 9 oz. There, you get an opportunity to set a world record and fish while doing it. It's not at all easy to get to Tree River. First you take a two-hour flight from Edmonton to Yellowknife in the Northwest Territories then Plummer's charter flight to Great Bear Lake is another hour. A second charter flight takes you from Great Bear Lake to Tree River in Nunavut. It is so far north the river flows only four miles before entering the Arctic Ocean and the sun never sets in the summer and never rises in the winter.

My friend Harold and I made that trip in June of 1985. Plummer's had a lodge on Great Bear Lake and another on Tree River. Although it is a very short season, the lodge is quite nice, and the meals are good. There are no fishing boats at the lodge as fishing is done from the shore of the river. My personal guide was a resident of Nunavut. At that time, they were called Eskimos. Today that word offends some and they are called Inuit. He didn't speak English and I wasn't sure if he understood it.

The first day he took me to a spot where the river flow was very fast. Using a rod and reel and lure, I spent the whole day casting and not catching. The lure would frequently get caught in the rocks of the fast-flowing river and for me, it seemed impossible to get loose. The guide could free it effortlessly, but he refused to show me how he did it.

He also showed no concern that I was not catching fish.

The second day started out no better than the first. Cast after cast and I got nothing. I knew it was very unlikely I would ever return and had no intention of not catching at least one char. Catching can sometimes be important! I told the guide, "I have never tipped a guide if no fish were caught."

We moved upstream less than a hundred yards and within an hour I had landed two: a fifteen and seventeen-pound Arctic char. Not a world record but my goal achieved.

I have never forgotten the raw beauty of the green tundra or the boat ride to the Arctic Ocean. In the fall the tundra turns red as does the belly of the arctic char, but our visit was in June. Some of the fellows jumped into the ocean just to say they had done it. I was satisfied with putting my hand in the water.

Fishing lodges are in business to make money to operate and having guests get fish mounted was one way of doing so. I agreed to have my fish mounted and proudly displayed it for years. At that time there was little or no thought to conservation. I have not had a lodge suggest getting a fish mounted in the last two decades.

Arctic Char from Tree River

6

NEGRO RIVER, MANAUS, BRAZIL

Peacock Bass

"Brian, this is Don Oborowski calling to see if you want to go fishing with me."

I had seen Don at various functions but had never formally met him, so it seemed strange that he would be asking me to go fishing.

I replied, "Can't you find anybody else?"

He said, "No."

He was planning a trip to Manaus, Brazil to catch peacock bass. I had never heard of peacock bass but was familiar with Manaus. In the late 1800's, Manaus had been the rubber capital of the world. Unfortunately, the industry was mismanaged and when rubber plant seeds were given to the Queen of England, the British Empire soon controlled the world rubber supply. Henry Ford invested over $30 million to build a 'city' called 'Fordlandia' on the Amazon. It was to supply all the rubber needed for his cars, but the venture failed. Having spent years in the tire business, this sounded like a fascinating trip, so I agreed to go.

It would not be a short trip. First, we took a 3 ½ hour flight from Edmonton to Toronto. From there to Miami is another flight of just over three hours. After overnighting in Miami, we caught the five-hour flight to Manaus. Having fun can be hard work.

Representatives from River Plate Anglers took us to the Zoological Manaus Tropical Hotel.

It was large and old, but it had clean rooms and great service. After a good rest we had breakfast and headed to the airport to catch a flight to our 'floating camp.' Our float plane delivered us right to our 'River Train.'

The camp consisted of four floating guest tents, various support tents, and boats to tow the train and to fish. The guest cabins had two single beds, private full bathrooms and were fully carpeted and nicely decorated. The 12' x 23' dining lounge tent served meals on linen tablecloths and the food was regional dishes. Breads and pastries were made daily and chilled wine, beer and Brazilian style margaritas were served daily. This was definitely my idea of roughing it!

The world record peacock bass is 28 pounds. They are known for their strength, so we brought special rods and reels with 80 lb. test line. Our guide spoke only Portuguese but was very knowledgeable about fishing. We left the 'train' in the morning and would meet it downriver at the end of the day.

The water is dark, and we never saw birds on the water. We were told it would not be good for their survival. Once we found an acceptable spot we would cast from the boat. We used what are called, 'woodchopper' lures. They float and have a propeller on one end. The noise, when you reel them in, attracts the fish. We were told if we saw bubbles in the water it indicates a female protecting her young. A cast into these bubbles almost always resulted in a fish.

The company brochure said we'd be in water 'never fished before,' and I believe it. Our guide used a machete to clear trees so we could get to a lagoon, the first of several we would visit.

Our group consisted of us and six men from Texas. We shared drinks and meals with them and of course, fish stories. Jimmy Cahill, from Sonora Texas, invited us to his game farm for turkey hunting. We took him up on it, but that is a story for later. Our group caught over 200 peacock bass with Don and I catching our share. They are a very colourful fish with three black stripes on a yellow or orange background.

Besides the fishing, our other highlight was the night sky, the downpour of rain, resting on hammocks tied to trees on shore at lunch time, and the beauty of the rainforest. I ignored advice to bring a flashlight, and I paid the price. It was so pitch black at night you could not walk the 200 feet back to your tent. without a flashlight. Sometimes, you should follow recommendations.

I never noticed any bugs during our trip. However, I was reading a hardcover book called, House of Morgan, about the American banking family. Each night in bed I would read for a while and then set my book on the floor. While unpacking after the trip, I noticed something had eaten the edges of several pages. I'm glad I didn't notice that at the time.

***

On my second trip to the Negro, I traveled with some acquaintances from Edmonton and their friends from Toronto. We stayed in the same hotel but fished on a yacht called Captain Peacock. They had phoned and recommended that our trip be rescheduled because of high water. Our 'leader' decided we would go anyway. Our group of eight caught a total of 32 fish in a week, rather than 200 like we did the first time.

While the fishing was slow, I caught my biggest peacock bass to date, a 20-pounder, the biggest catch anyone made on either trip. I also caught my first piranha which we ate on the shore for lunch. It's much better you eat them than them eating you.

On my first trip here, I had seen an attractive H Stern Watch for sale in the hotel lobby. H Stern specializes in luxury jewelry. I was reaching that age where I needed reading glasses. I had a gold watch and now I struggled to see the hands on it, but this watch had a blue back and gold hands, making it easy to see. It was nice looking, I really wanted it, but I let the price stop me, and I regretted it. This time I was not going to feel remorse for such a decision. More than a decade later, I still wear that watch.

For my third visit to the Negro, Fred and Shirley Helmer invited Wynne and me to join them on a riverboat fishing trip. We flew to Manaus through Atlanta, stayed at the same hotel, then flew to a place called Barcelos where we boarded a riverboat with several others. Again, the fishing was great as was the experience. A highlight of this trip was a boat tour to see the dark Rio Negro water meet the sandy coloured river called Solimoes to form the Amazon River. The rivers' water runs side by side without mixing for a couple of miles. Half the river is gold, and half the river is black. It reminded me of Alberta where we call oil black gold.

You could fish the Rio Negro a hundred times and have a hundred unique experiences. I was lucky enough to have three.

River train on Negro River, Brazil

First piranha I caught- great lunch

Resting in Amazon Rain Forest

Peacock Bass are beautiful fish

7

DEVILS RIVER, TEXAS

Bass

I would never have thought that fishing in Brazil would result in my fishing in Devils River in Southern Texas, but it did. Jimmy Cahill lived in Sonora, Texas and his family was well known and had a long history there. Sonora is a couple hour drive west of San Antonio and has a population of about 3,000. It is where in 1901, Sheriff E. S. Bryant shot William Carver, a member of Butch Cassidy's Hole-in-the-Wall Gang. It was also home of Dan Blocker, who played Hoss on the television show Bonanza.

Jimmy had invited Don and I to his lodge to hunt wild turkey. I am not a hunter but had some experience in Canada hunting ducks, geese, and pheasants so agreed to go. I hunted turkey three times, including once with my son-in-law, Rynhard. I didn't shoot a turkey until my third trip but enjoyed the experience much more than the hunting.

Jimmy was a great host and took me on a tour of the area including a tour of the Caverns of Sonora. The caverns run along a fault, where gases mixed with acidic water to form the caverns. While not the largest, the Caverns of Sonora have lots of steps, and you get close views of the unique formations. They are recognized as one of the most beautiful show caves on earth and they lived up to the reputation.

I prefer fishing over hunting, so when Jimmy offered to go fishing for bass on the Devils River, I jumped at the opportunity. The river starts in southwestern Texas and drains into the Rio Grande, near the Mexican border. It is considered one of the most unspoiled rivers in Texas. The river flows underground for part of its journey. As it passes underground, the gravel, sand, and limestone clean the water before it re-emerges some 20 miles downstream.

Jimmy was receiving oil royalties, some which might have come from his property along this river. Unlike in Canada where most of the oil rights are owned by the government in Texas individuals have ownership. We entered a private road ignoring a warning sign of the Gulf Oil Corporation and spent the night at a comfortable cabin and set out the next morning for the river. Don and his son Shawn were in a pickup with Jimmy, while I rode in a pickup with a friend of his. I couldn't believe the poor quality of the road leading down into the canyon where the river flowed. There were no guard rails, and if you slipped off the edge, you had no hope for survival. The trip became much more treacherous when my driver friend told me he had just spent a million dollars on a heart transplant.

I prayed it was money well spent.

We finally arrived at the fishing spot. Only then did I discover we would each have a kayak for an all-day paddling adventure down the river to where someone would meet us with overnight supplies. I don't swim well nor am I one to kayak. Within minutes I had tipped over, gotten soaked, lost my sunglasses, but thankfully I survived and still had my camera and other items in a floating waterproof bag.

Wonderful sights awaited us. The landscape was breathtaking and we even saw a coyote 'herding' a flock of sheep. To avoid rapids, everyone except Shawn portaged their kayak to safer water. Shawn, who is a diabetic and lives every day like it might be his last, decided to go over the fall. It worked brilliantly until he flipped his kayak and lost his fishing rod and insulin supplies. Much to my surprise, they dove in and retrieved both from the river.

We floated by a huge development at the top of the canyon. I noticed it when a private jet landed on the air strip. Somebody had a lot of money. According to Jimmy, the State of Texas sued the tobacco manufacturers and were awarded a settlement of over $15 billion dollars, with five lawyers charging a fee of $5 billion, but only received $3.3 billion, still certainly enough for one of them to own this property.

We were so focused on navigating, we very seldom put a hook in the water, which explains why we were skunked. I was so relieved when we agreed that one day was more than enough. Rather than overnight on the banks of the river we mercifully went back to the cabin. I should have known unguided fishing trips are not for me.

8

FRASER RIVER, BRITISH COLUMBIA

Sturgeon

The Fraser River flows 1,375 kilometres from the Rocky Mountains into the Pacific Ocean at Vancouver, making it the longest river in British Columbia. It is also the best river for fishing for sturgeon in Canada. Sturgeon are an historic fish that date back centuries.

They are a protected species in Canada, but you can catch and release. A sturgeon has a dorsal fin similar to a shark and an elongated, spindle-like, scaleless body covered with five lateral rows of bony plates called scutes. They can live for decades, grow to twelve feet, and weigh hundreds of pounds. They are a potential source of caviar which is a reason they are on the endangered list.

Rick Hansen and Fred Helmer were instrumental in establishing a 'tagging' program for the sturgeon in the Fraser River. Guided fishing trips scan sturgeon caught to see if they are tagged. If they are tagged, guides measure the size of the fish and identify the location it was caught. If the fish had been tagged, they will tell you where, when, and size at that time.

If the fish hasn't been tagged the guide will insert a tag in the gill. Over 100,000 fish have been tagged to date.

I met Fred Helmer through meeting Rick Hansen. Rick was in an automobile accident when he was fifteen that left him a paraplegic. From March 21, 1985 to May22, 1987 he wheeled through 34 countries on his 'Man in Motion' tour which raised funds, awareness, and helped show the world the potential of people with disabilities. He wheeled the distance of the circumference of the world on this tour. He has dedicated his life to making the world a better place for people with disabilities and is a Canadian hero. He is also the most avid fisherman I know.

Fred owned a tackle shop just east of Vancouver in Chilliwack, BC. He also owned a business that did guided sturgeon fishing trips. Rick sponsored a fundraising salmon fishing tournament every year and Fred volunteered to be one of the guides for the event. He was my guide the first year I attended the tournament.

My first sturgeon fishing trip with Fred was with friends Craig, Vern and Jim. We booked a two-day trip hoping to at least catch one sturgeon. Fred's boat provided protection from the elements and easily accommodated four guests and himself. We head out on the river to a spot where Fred anchors the boat. For bait, we use salmon fish eggs wrapped in a women's nylon stocking. The ball of bait is attached to a hook and cast in the water where it sinks to the bottom. The four fishing rods are left in holders until you see a bend in the rod.

That's when the excitement begins. These fish can be enormous, and they often breach the water in their fight for freedom. Once the fish is landed it is checked for a tag, if none, a tag is placed on the fish after taking its measurements. If tagged, the guide can get you previous information on the fish. We caught over thirty fish on that first trip.

On another trip I hooked a large one, and Fred immediately got me a belt with provision to hold the rod. I saw the line coming toward the surface and knew the fish was about to clear the water. It was a monster! Battle time is often difficult to gauge, but I must have fought it for close to an hour. When the battle ended the fish was tired and there was no fight left and there was also no fight left in me. Who says fishing is not exercise? We towed it to shore, and according to measurements Fred said it weighed 375 pounds. The biggest fish I ever caught by more than one hundred pounds. My brother Morris also caught his largest fish on a sturgeon fishing trip with me and Ernie Wiggins.

***

Another time, David, my friend Craig's son, and I went fishing with Rick Hansen. David was then a PhD engineering student and was researching an item to measure the stress you could put on the spine during surgery. Rick was aware of similar research and they spent some of the day discussing that, and its potential long-term prognosis for those with spinal cord injuries.

Driving to the boat, Rick had asked me if I was interested in accompanying him on a trip to China. The event was to celebrate the 25th anniversary of his Man in Motion tour. I knew his adventure had inspired Canadian David Foster, and English singer John Parr, to compose 'St. Elmo's Fire' (Man In Motion), giving the tour a theme song. I didn't know he and his team were visiting several countries to celebrate the 25th anniversary of the tour. I accepted his offer and spent ten wonderful days with his contingent in China. We were well received and were on the Great Wall of China in the spring of 2011, exactly twenty-five years to the day of his tour visit in 1986. From the original team of six, four made the second trip with us, along with his daughter, a TV crew, and support staff. Stops included Beijing, Shanghai, and Hong Kong. Ten of the most memorable days of my life and all because of relationships made fishing.

The third most memorable sturgeon trip was when we took the Rankel family on a sturgeon fishing trip. Their fifteen-year old son Noah was at that age where you can spend your time doing activities that can be wrong life choices. Taking up fishing in the Saskatchewan River in Edmonton was a very wise decision he made. Inviting me to join him and his Dad was an appreciated gesture. He was thrilled when I invited his family for a two-day sturgeon fishing trip. He displayed no frustration despite getting skunked the first day. The next day, his patience paid off when he landed a very large sturgeon. I was in the boat but did not fish. That I didn't catch a fish didn't matter. I believe you have arrived as a true fisherman when you get more enjoyment out of seeing another person's excitement at catching a fish than catching one yourself.

Craig and Brian with Craig's sturgeon

Jim, Brian and Craig with Brian's sturgeon

thanks
for a great day
on the water!

Rick Hansen, Brian and David Benfield fishing in the snow

9

TRINITY RIVER, TEXAS

Gar

When most people hear of Waco, Texas they think of the Branch Davidian siege. The standoff lasted from February 28-April 19, 1993. The Bureau of Alcohol, Tobacco and Firearms (BATF) suspected the religious group of stockpiling illegal weapons, so they obtained a search warrant for the compound and arrest warrants for Koresh and a handful of members. When BATF attempted to serve a search and arrest warrant on the ranch, a gunfight erupted, resulting in the deaths of four government agents and six Branch Davidians. It ended when law enforcement attacked the building resulting in a fire that destroyed the building, killing 76 people. including 25 children and cult leader, David Koresh.

To me, Waco is the city where my daughter Allison and her husband Rynhard lived for several years. My three grandchildren Juliette, Brianna, and Joshua were all born in Waco. Predictably, I made frequent visits there. I toured the factory where all the Snickers bars in North America are made; the Dr. Pepper Museum, which honours the popular drink invented in Waco, and the Texas Ranger Hall of Fame and Museum, where I was pleased to see they recognized, "Walker, Texas Ranger". I was surprised to see a Royal Canadian Mounted Police uniform on display. The RCMP and Rangers are the only group that can enforce federal, provincial, state, and municipal laws.

Allison and I also visited the Branch Davidian site which is supposedly now run by a Canadian. There is a memorial with all the names of everyone who died there. It's surreal to be standing at a site so many lives, including children, were taken. We took a picture in front of the memorial but left when we saw people coming out of the building. They were quite far away, but we didn't wish to speak to anybody.

We also visited the site of George W Bush's ranch. When his term was up in 2008, the first place he spoke was Edmonton, Alberta. I attended and met him at a pre-event reception where I had my picture taken with him. I told him my daughter lived in Waco and he said, "You should visit the ranch next time you are in town". I told him "We did stop by and your security people told us to leave". He laughed.

One day, Rynhard called me and said, "Would you like to go fishing for alligator gar?"

I had never heard of them but readily agreed to give it a try. The fish gets its name from its long head, slender body, and razor-sharp teeth. At ten feet they can weigh upwards of 300 pounds, it's one of the largest freshwater fish in America, and it's considered a delicacy in parts of the south.

He booked a guided trip and we headed off to a spot on the Trinity River to meet our guide near Palestine, about a two-hour drive east of Waco. The Trinity River is over seven hundred miles long, so good directions were essential. Our guide's name was Bubba, the same as a character in the movie, "Forrest Gump." The movie character became so popular, that a Bubba Gump Shrimp Company Seafood Restaurant chain was formed. The Bubba in the movie was Black so I was surprised our Bubba guide was brown and he was a third-generation Texan. I don't know his given name, but he told us his grandfather gave him the name as a child, and it stuck. He would have had the name long before the movie.

My stereotype thinking really made me question my bias. If I thought a person named Bubba would be Black from watching a movie, would I think someone from Palestine, Texas would be a brown coloured person? It made me much more conscious of the effort required to rid myself of prejudice. Fishing teaches you more than how to fish.

✳✳✳

I had wondered about the method to be used for catching alligator gar, and I never would have guessed. First, Bubba baited and cast the lines, then secured the fishing rods in the mud along the shore. We then took the boat downstream and relaxed while waiting for a sensor to sound, telling us we hooked a fish. This was more technology than I had ever used while fishing. Not much later we heard the sensor, and we were off to grab the rod.

Normally, you will 'set' the hook as soon as a fish takes it, but that's not how you catch gar. They take the bait and run downstream before crossing to the other side of the river. They then come back upstream to the original spot where they had taken the bait.

We must have spent fifteen minutes watching the float move in the water before Bubba said, "Set the hook now."

I did so, and started reeling it in. Bubba said, "It looks like we caught a junior." Suddenly, when the fish got close to the boat, it took off, almost taking me with it. My arms were tired, and the adrenalin was flowing when I finally landed a very large alligator gar.

But catching the fish was not our only excitement. A large water moccasin jumped out of the water right into the boat. I didn't realize it was a pit viper that, although they seldom bite, can be very dangerous. I'm not really afraid of snakes, since we don't really have any in Canada. But Rynhard and Bubba knew all about it. I think Rynhard just kicked it off the boat. There was really no time to panic.

Bubba said my fish was over seven feet long and weighed two hundred and forty pounds. Rynhard caught a fish that was over six feet long and weighed one hundred sixty-five pounds.

The Texas State and world record for an alligator gar caught on a rod and reel is 279 pounds so we didn't break the record. Bubba may have stretched the truth about the size, but they were big fish. A day I will never forget.

Brian and Rynhard with their gar

Guess which gar is Brian's catch?

10

RIVER FISHING, 'ON THE FLY'

Cutthroat trout, brown trout

The popular movie, "A River Runs Through It" starred Brad Pitt and positively portrayed fly fishing. Watching a person cast a fly line on a river makes many fishermen dream of doing it. Fly fishing is with a rod and reel just as is fishing with a lure. The difference is the weight of the fishing line, which creates the distance cast, whereas in traditional fishing, the lure's weight gives casting distance. Many more hours are spent perfecting how to cast with flies than with lures. A good fly fisherman can cast the fly to a very specific location.

Try as I might to become a successful fly fisherman, it never happened. I had no interest in studying and making my own flies. Nor did I have any interest in becoming an expert at casting. "River Monsters", a TV series on catching large fish was of much more interest to me. My lack of desire to learn this admirable skill may be a result of the simple fishing methods used in my youth. Fishing, to me, should be a simple outing not a complex one. Fly fishing is interesting to me but not very appealing.

My lack of interest in fly fishing was not without effort. At a Trout Unlimited fundraiser, I purchased a one-week guided package at Elkford, British Columbia. The package was for two people and included a condominium in Elkford. Elkford is about a seven-hour drive southwest of Edmonton in the southeast part of B.C. It developed primarily because of area coal mines but today it's a town popular for outdoor recreational activities.

The two men who had donated the trip were very avid fly fishermen. Each owned a condominium in Elkford. Wynne and I stayed in one, and the owner bunked in with his friend. Our condo had fly-fishing wallpaper, fly-fishing pictures on the wall, even fly-fishing dishes, and dishcloths. One of them had even authored a huge, hardcover book on the "Mayfly", an insect often used for fly fishing as they are an important food for trout.

Wynne and I soon discovered the difference between being a great fisherman and a great guide. They gave us some basic instructions and then we each partnered with one of them, jumped in a truck and drove from stream to stream to fly fish. Wynne's guide made her feel so incompetent she took the bus home on the third day. I had paid for a week and was determined to get full value.

The fish weren't biting, and my guide kept saying "You missed that one."

Finally, I asked him to show me how to do it, I then kept saying to him, "You missed that one."

We agreed it would be better if I fished alone for a while.

It is a beautiful setting with the mountains and the river. Sitting on the shore, it dawned on me I had nothing to think about. I had just stepped down as CEO of the Fountain Tire Company and worried about having nothing to do. My plans for the next twelve months had an adventure every month. July was this trip. Sitting alone it occurred to me I had focused on planning my physical time rather than planning for my mental free time. That was the moment I decided I would write books. Once again, my life had purpose.

Pat, a good friend of mine from student days, gave up golf and took up fly fishing. When he develops an interest, he goes all out. He took courses on fly fishing, built a beautiful cabin near the Rocky Mountains, and learned how to make his own flies. He took me fly fishing on more than one occasion, including trips to his cabin and Montana. In Montana we certainly caught fish, but the trip is more remembered for a shore lunch. The chairs our guide provided were not stable and mine collapsed causing me to hit my tailbone on a rock. The healing process was not rapid and on my trip to France later that fall, I couldn't drive a car because of the pain. Who knew you could get hurt fishing?

Mike, another friend, also took me fly fishing. Although

I enjoyed it, it always made me think salmon fishing was much more exciting, at least for me.

Fly fishing in the Saskatchewan River

Proof of catching a fish 'on the fly'

LAKES

1

DILLBERRY LAKE, ALBERTA

Rainbow Trout

Dillberry Lake lies on the border of Alberta and Saskatchewan with half of the lake in each province. The lake in Alberta lies within the Dillberry Lake Provincial Park which is close to the town of Provost. In 1971 I was teaching high school in Provost and staying at the home of Wally and Lynne Herle, and their two young sons. They lived in the farmhouse where Wally grew up. Wally also taught and I was fortunate to room and board with them.

Their friends became my friends.

One winter evening after school, Wally, Roland, Dwight, and I left the farm to go ice fishing at Dillberry Lake. It was stocked with rainbow trout. I knew it might be quite an experience because Roland and Dwight had once stopped at the farm when we were having breakfast. They said they had been ice fishing and were just getting home.

When I asked, "Didn't you get any sleep?" Roland, who spoke very slowly replied, "Well, not last night."

Ice fishing at Dillberry was not sitting outside freezing. There was a fish hut that was left on the ice all winter, and it could be towed to different fishing spots. It was taken home before the ice melted in the spring.

The hut had a heater and chairs. An ice auger was used to drill fishing holes. We put a kernel of corn on a bare hook and dropped the line in the water. You could tend your line or just watch for a bite. We didn't catch a lot, but we weren't skunked either. Time flies when you are having fun and we were very late getting back to the farm.

The next morning Wally and I each commented on how good we felt with so little sleep. We had lots of time and didn't rush to school. However, when we arrived, it looked like we were late. We were.

We'd checked the electric clock on the wall at home without realizing the power had been off for a couple of hours, and it was closer to eleven than nine. The other teachers were enjoying our feeble excuse for being late. When the principal came into the staff room and heard our story he asked, "When did you realize you were late?" He often took the liberty of coming late himself, so I replied, "When I saw your car in the parking lot." The laughter suddenly turned to him. The staff room experience was as memorable as the fishing experience.

2

LAKE WABAMUN, ALBERTA

Northern Pike

Lake Wabamun lies about an hour west of Edmonton. I never understood why we called it Lake Wabamun rather than Wabamun Lake. I don't really know why 'lake' precedes or follows the name of any particular lake. It was originally called White Whale Lake because of the large whitefish caught in its waters. I don't know when it became known as Wabamun which is a Cree word meaning 'mirror'.

Since the 60's, my father-in-law, Wally, had owned a cabin at Seba Beach, a village on the lake. The cabin had a boat and I fished from a boat for the first time in memory. I spent many hours fishing for pike or 'jack' fish as we called them. One day I was catching fish after fish and Keith, my brother-in-law, was catching nothing. We finally decided to go to the store and get him the same lure I was using. When we got back to the same spot neither of us caught anything. I never again doubted the importance of the difference one type of lure or bait could have over another on any given day.

My daughter Allison caught her first fish on that lake. She was six and was excited about going fishing but worried that we might be fishing from a catamaran sailboat rather than a motorboat. I suspect her uncle planted that idea in her head. My brother-in-law Keith and I had agreed to take his two children, Erin and RJ and my daughter fishing. Erin was a bit older than Allison and RJ a bit younger. She hooked her first fish. I was very proud of how she kept her composure landing it. I thought she would feel sorry for the fish and want to put it back, but I couldn't have been more wrong. She wanted to get back to the cabin to clean and cook the fish. Like father, like daughter, she wanted someone else to clean the fish and do the cooking. I recall it being one of the best fish I ever tasted. Allison is now married with three young children and still loves to fish.

***

I went ice fishing more than once at Lake Wabamun. We used individual fish tents rather than fish huts. My clothes and body heat provided me with warmth. We would find a good place to fish, drill holes in the ice, and each of us would set our tent up over the hole, protected from the wind and to a degree, from the cold. Unlike catching pike in the summer, we caught white fish in the winter.

Sometimes, fishermen don't follow, or maybe they just don't understand, fishing etiquette.

Wabamun is a big lake, but others would set up right next to our spot. I disliked the violation of our privacy and suggested we set up in a place we knew had no fish.

We did, and sure enough, we soon had company right next door. Fortunately, we had not drilled holes, so we just packed up and moved to a place we knew had fish. The group didn't follow us so they likely got skunked. People can sometimes be very predictable.

My final memory of fishing at Lake Wabamun was when my friend Pat booked a fly fishing day at the lake. He invited me to join him. I am no expert at fly fishing but had a very enjoyable day and even caught some pike 'on the fly.'

I probably spent more hours fishing on Lake Wabamun than any other lake. It was a great way to relax during the years I spent studying to become an accountant and for years after I began my career.

Keith Eccles with Allison, R.J. and Erin

Allison a little older, still fishing

3

GULL LAKE, LACOMBE ALBERTA

Whitefish

Leroy Hawtin, a former business partner, invited Allison, Rynhard and I out to ice fishing at Gull Lake. Gull Lake is about 149 km south of Edmonton near the town of Lacombe. Lacombe is the home of Len Thompson fishing lures, popular among fishermen.

The town has the world's largest fishing lure displaying the yellow and red five of diamonds pattern, his most popular hook. Leroy lives in Lacombe and had all the necessary supplies. We met him at his home and headed out to the lake. If you have never driven on ice and come from South Africa, hearing ice crack under your vehicle can make one a bit nervous. We weren't nervous and didn't realize Rynhard was! Once we arrived at the 'spot,' Leroy unloaded the fold-up hut from the back of the truck, set it up and used an ice auger to make fishing holes. Once we have our lines in the water there is nothing to do but enjoy the hot chocolate he provided and wait for the fish.

Allison caught a fish just when Leroy looked outside and saw the game warden had arrived in the area. Since she didn't have a license, he suggested she forget the fish. That wasn't going to happen. Despite Leroy's warning, she proceeded to land the fish. Leroy commented, "The acorn doesn't fall far from the tree!"

That was a Sunday that Rynhard will remember the most but also will not be forgotten by Allison and myself. It was a reminder how fortunate we are in Canada to be able to fish in each of the distinct seasons. Ice fishing is much more popular in Canada than it is in Mexico.

Ice fishing hut at Gull Lake

Allison caught a fish

4

ANDREW LAKE LODGE, ALBERTA

Lake Trout and Northern Pike

Andrew Lake is in the northeast corner of Alberta near the border of the NWT and Saskatchewan. It is a several hours flight from Edmonton and is only accessible by air. I came to know of the lodge in the late 1970's through a business relationship. The fishing lodge was a client of our accounting firm. I visited the lodge a couple of times, once in an amphibious flying seaplane that was a cargo plane. It had no seats or insulation, making it cold, noisy, and uncomfortable. The washroom was a bucket in the back of the plane. Who says money can't buy happiness? The flight was a memorable experience especially when water began leaking through the rivet holes when the plane landed on the water.

Thankfully, the lodge was comfortable, and the boats were fine. Everyone was anxious to start fishing, but we had to learn the rules and receive fishing tips. Since it is so far north, you could fish in sunlight for almost twenty-four hours. However, we had no guides, and we could only use barbless hooks. They emphasized that this was a trophy lake and catch and release was encouraged. This was my introduction to barbless hooks and the concept of catch and release.

The best fishing, as usual, was said to be on the far side of the lake. It was a big lake, and that advice was of little benefit. The few trout we caught certainly didn't qualify as 'trophies,' but the trip was fun. We were introduced to shore lunches which included making a fire and frying fresh fish.

A great memory was Ernie telling me, "You left the door open this morning when you stopped to ask us if we were going fishing."

I replied, "I saw a mosquito in your cabin, and I thought I would let it out." Apparently, it didn't leave and instead, invited many more friends into the cabin.

The lodge got into financial trouble in the economic downturn in the early 1980's. I was offered a ten percent interest in the lodge for zero cost. I never regretted my decision to reject that offer. Fishing lodges and golf courses are best used rather than owned. Some of my best deals were the ones I didn't do.

5

POTTS LAKE, ALBERTA LAKE

Trout and Northern Pike

Potts Lake is situated at the northeast corner of Alberta, near the borders of the Northwest Territories and Saskatchewan, and that's where Keith Eccles, Ron Young, Jim Pangle and I were dropped off for a four-day fishing adventure. Why does one think the more remote and farther from home you fish, the greater the odds of catching the 'big one.'

We brought our own tackle and gear; the tent and boats were supplied. When you book these kinds of places you don't know what you are getting. The pictures are often more flattering than the real accommodations, so let's just say the tents were more rustic than we were led to believe.

The boats were fine. Jim and I fished in one and the other two in another. We were the only boats on the lake. Jim drove our boat and somehow got our lines tangled with the lines of Keith and Ron. With only two boats on the entire lake it makes you wonder why people do the things they do.

One night, Keith and Ron decided to sleep under the stars. A great idea if not for the armies of mosquitoes and black flies. Despite their creative protective netting, before long they came rushing into the tent accompanied by hundreds of bugs. Nature can be harsh.

This is where I saw the largest lake trout of all my fishing trips to the north. The way his rod bent, Jim thought he had snagged the lake's bottom, but he quickly realized he'd snagged a large fish. After a feisty battle, he had the fish near the boat. I grabbed the net to bring it in only to discover our hosts had supplied us with a net more suited to catch monarch butterflies. After a couple of unsuccessful netting attempts, we helplessly watched the big fish slowly swim away. It didn't seem to appease Jim when I explained that he had experienced all the thrill of fishing EXCEPT for bragging rights. Nobody believes a story of the 'big one' that got away.

We were relieved when the plane arrived to take us home. I was beginning to think 'roughing it' was not my cup of tea.

6

NONACHO LAKE , NWT

Lake Trout and Northern Pike

Nonacho Lake is the eighth largest lake in the Northwest Territories; north of Yellowknife, it stretches over two hundred miles. It's a fly-in only experience since the nearest highway is two hundred miles away. There are no telephones or internet, and you will see no-one on the lake other than other lodge guests. The six cabins can accommodate four to eight people. They are furnished and have electricity. You must bring your own fishing gear, but sixteen-foot Lund Boats are provided.

We made two trips to this lake although I am not sure why we returned. We caught fish, but when asking my fellow fishermen their memories of Nonacho Lake, none mentioned catching lake trout or northern pike. All complained of the black flies and the mosquitos. Mosquitoes usually won't bother you while fishing on the water, but while in his boat, Ron remembers them covering his hands, his only body part not protected by clothing or netting.

Murray only remembers Craig telling owner Merlin Carter as he left to "Have a good life." His sarcastic tone signaled we would not be back. Sadly, in June 2005, Myles Carter found his father's body at the lodge sight. He had been killed by a bear. They believed Merlin was attacked in the dark, and that his flashlight either scared the bear or made it feel threatened. We knew the camp had a bug problem, but we never thought it might also have a bear problem.

More and more it seemed like I was not intended to land a large lake trout or northern pike.

Although we had given up on Nonacho Lake, we decided to try the North Star Resort on Thekuthili Lake, which is only about 100 km from Nonacho. Like Nonacho, you had to fly in by float plane. Once again, the accommodation and boats were fine. Once again, we caught fish, but nothing significant. I thought this would be my last trip to a fishing camp in the NWT. The beauty of the environment and clear blue waters of the lakes did not outweigh my dislike for the bugs and lack of fishing success.

Brian holding a northern pike

Too much bug protection required for a fun time

7

GREAT BEAR LAKE

Trout and Grayling

I read about a fishing trip where a jet landed on a dirt runway taking guests to a fishing lodge in the Northwest Territories to catch lake trout, northern pike, and grayling, I decided to go but only if I could find a friend to join me. It wouldn't be easy due to its cost and the trip lasting a week. Then I heard the magic words. "I would love to go."

I couldn't believe it.

Harold Greenwood, who I first met in 1976 at Fountain Tire, had just agreed to go fishing at Plummer's Lodge. I had known Harold as his auditor for eight years before buying an interest in the company and becoming his partner in 1984. He surprised me because he had few social contacts with anyone from Fountain Tire. He had never expressed any more interest in fishing than he had in golf or any sport.

Great Bear Lake is the fourth largest lake in North America, and only sees about 300 anglers a year. The lake's size makes a guide necessary. The facilities are very comfortable and the orientation presentation informative. It is an unforgettable experience landing on a dirt runway with a commercial size aircraft.

We were briefed on the rules, hours of fishing and introduced to our guides. I was surprised the guests could drink while fishing and could give beer, but not hard liquor, to the guides. A couple of guests ignored the warning of not giving alcohol to their guide. It is a large lake, and the guide couldn't find his way back to the lodge. They spent the night under the stars on the shore which exposed them to the elements and the bugs. In my mind the lodge didn't demonstrate integrity when they fired the guide rather than reprimand the guests.

They also said we could pay extra to take a float plane to another lake, which would improve our chances of catching bigger fish. I would have done that in a heartbeat, but Harold didn't want to spend the extra money, so we declined. We had a good guide and caught lake trout but not large ones. I also caught my first graylings but was more focused on catching the big one. We had impressive numbers but failed at landing big ones.

I wasn't surprised or happy to learn the two guys who paid to fish from the float plane had each caught a trout weighing in at over 50 pounds. They had fished by casting from the pontoons of the float plane. What a missed opportunity.

It had been a very enjoyable trip with nice weather. It was also a valuable learning experience. I vowed to never rationalize missing an opportunity by saving a dollar.

8

CREE LAKE, SASKATCHEWAN

Lake Trout and Northern Pike

I couldn't believe my good fortune when I found a lodge that offered a direct flight from Edmonton to Cree Lake in Northern Saskatchewan. They boasted of having monster pike and huge lake trout as well as Arctic grayling and walleye. The lodge arranged the flight and provided cabin accommodation and boats. We had to bring groceries, beverages, fishing gear, sleeping bags and toiletries.

I called Craig, Vern and Jim and we were soon off to Cree Lake. Craig has constantly bored us with discussing the 'best' fishing trip ever being at Russell Lake in Northern Saskatchewan. We were now heading to Northern Saskatchewan to hopefully put that fish story to rest.

We headed out in late September for the last trip of the year for the lodge. We preferred battling cold rather than bugs. The flight, including the landing on a dirt runway, cabins and boats were much better than expected. The fishing was good, but not great with neither monster pike nor huge lake trout being caught. We never even tried to catch grayling or walleye.

A strange memory from this trip was a group of four hunters staying at the lodge.

One of them shot a moose on the other side of the lake. It was going to be a lot of work to bring it back to the camp. They returned and asked us if we would help them bring it back to the cabin. Since it wasn't close to Christmas, we declined their kind offer.

We were ready to leave when the plane arrived to take us home. We were worried when they told us they might not have room for all of us. We were relieved when they informed us that we could leave, if we agreed to have our fish returned on a separate flight.

However, when the fish arrived Craig neglected to pick it up at the warehouse. The fish spoiled! Had I told Craig the cost per pound of that fish he might have changed his plans. I believe the trip was more memorable than the one he had in Russell Lake. I haven't heard about it since our trip.

We made one last attempt to catch a large Northern Pike at a lodge near Fort McMurray, the home of the Canadian Oil Sands. Upon arrival I almost immediately caught a good-sized fish. Our anticipation did not last long. Due to a lack of snow cover on the ice, we were told the lake had frozen to the bottom, killing all the large fish. We spent the next few days catching two-pound pike on a 30-pound test line. We could have stayed home and fished in a goldfish bowl for as much excitement.

9

GREAT SLAVE LAKE

Trout Northern Pike

Yellowknife, the capital of the NWT, lies on the north shore of Great Slave Lake. It is the second largest lake in the NWT after Great Bear Lake and the tenth largest in the world. It is known for large lake trout, northern pike, and grayling. My older brother Clayton and I took a two-hour flight from Edmonton to Yellowknife. Driving would have taken us over sixteen hours.

We met up with a local business owner and Ozzie who was a representative for a supplier to our company. I didn't know him well and had never met our host. Our spirits soared as we set out on his very nice, well-equipped boat. The weather was beautiful, the scenery spectacular, and the sun never set. As expected, the fish were some distance from our starting point.

We finally arrived at our campsite, a secluded spot with a large flat rock to set out the tent. We were surprised when there was no indication we would be fishing. Instead the plan seemed to be to have a few drinks and then have a few more drinks with no thought of taking the boat out. Not the program we had been promised.

Clayton and I decided to cast from shore to see if any fish were around. The 'big one' landed was at least one pound. I got a picture of him holding it. This was not going to be a good fishing trip.

While heading home a highlight was when the host explained how he had emergency cans of gas stored at different locations along the shore. Then we saw a boat leaving the general area. They must have also been short of gas because our host found his cache to be gone.

We were relieved to finally check into the motel for some well-deserved sleep and relaxation. Suddenly the phone rang. We'd been invited to the host's home for dinner.

We accepted and it turned out to be like being with different people. A very enjoyable evening.

Great memories yes, fish no.

Clayton and Brian Hesje with single fish caught

10

KLUANE WILDERNESS LODGE, YUKON, CANADA

Lake Trout and Northern Pike

I couldn't resist when Don called and asked me to join him on a trip to Kluane Lodge in the Yukon. I had a goal of visiting all ten provinces and three territories in Canada and Yukon had not been visited. The flight from Edmonton to Whitehorse, the capital of the Yukon Territory is almost 2,000 km. north west. A float plane then takes you 260 km to the lodge, and gives you a spectacular view of Mount Logan, the highest peak in Canada. The accommodations, boats and meals were of very high quality.

The lodge offered no guides, and Don paired me up with one of his employees. It is a long day fishing with someone who has very different interests. He was not a great fisherman nor was he a great boat handler. I told him that buoys near the lodge warned you of the rocks. Either he didn't believe me or didn't understand, but regardless, he ignored my advice, and minutes later we had $500 plus damage to the motor. Entertaining for me but expensive for Don. He was so excited he stepped off the boat and landed in the water between the boat and the dock in four feet of cold water. He waited there while I went and got my camera. He was a standup comedian.

Brian Dack, who owns and manages the lodge, seemed to have no interest in telling us the spots to fish nor the lures to use. Predictably, few fish were caught. The area's beauty, seeing a moose on shore less than 100 feet away, and 24 hours of sunshine were memorable, the fishing was not.

Lack of fish did not mean lack of laughter. I went back a second time with the group. We had a great time in Whitehorse and at the lodge but my many failed attempts at catching a big trout or a big pike meant the end of my attempt to do so.

Shore lunches were great

11

LOUGH LEANE LAKE, KILLARNEY, IRELAND

Perch, Bass

Allison had earned a Bachelor's of Commerce from the University of Alberta in the late 1990's. After graduating she and her best friend Erin Guthrie moved to Ireland. They planned on only staying for one year. Erin, unfortunately, had been diagnosed with cancer at age eighteen but it was now in remission Thankfully they had many enjoyable years together in Ireland before she passed away.

I now had a reason to travel to Ireland and did so on more than one occasion. I couldn't believe Killarney had a Fishing and Golf Club. My two favourite pastimes! I played the golf course by myself and once again proved I can be alone and have a competition. I promised myself I would buy the crystal trophy I had seen in the pro shop if I made par on the eighteenth hole. Today it proudly sits in our Vegas condo.

My fishing experience had a much greater impact on my life than did my golf game. One day, I received a call from Allison saying she had a new 'friend' from South Africa that I should meet. She planned a fishing trip for us that included her new friend Rynhard. He seemed to be a nice young man even though he had a very heavy accent. I didn't have to be told his first language was not English. I had never known someone whose first language was Afrikaans.

We launched from Ross Castle and thankfully had a guide. I was told there were three lakes, and we would be fishing the lower lake called Lough Leane. I had no expectations of catching any fish, but the fishing was great. We caught perch and bass releasing some but keeping fish for dinner. I was happy to see Allison had become a bit like me. Use a guide and never touch a fish. When we got home, she suggested we go shopping for groceries. She was certainly not in a rush to get back. I soon discovered why.

Rynhard had not only cleaned the fish, he was also cooking them. A man who carries the fish home, cleans them, AND cooks them need do nothing more to gain my approval.

Today they are married and have three children. One day, I hope my grandchildren, Juliette, Brianna, and Joshua grow to love fishing.

Allison , Brian and Rynhard in Ireland

12

FISHING PARK, BANGKOK, THAILAND

Catfish

For a while, my brother Murray worked and lived in Thailand. He invited us to visit and he booked a fishing trip. The chartered trip didn't last long before turning around and heading for shore. I didn't experience sea sickness, but the others did. We were not destined to land any large fish.

Back in Bangkok, I booked a day of fishing at a fishing park which is a man-made lake inside the city. Our guide walked us to one of the many old wooden fishing huts on the water. He had the required fishing rods and reels. He also had the refreshments and a pail of mash. He took a handful of the mash and made it into a ball. He then put the hook in the ball and cast. Almost instantly a fish would be on the line. Soon Wynne and I were reeling in catfish after catfish. Of course, I wanted to catch a large one, and I soon got my wish. The fish's fight forced me out of the hut and past a bridge before I finally landed it. And what a monster, a 50 lb. catfish.

This was one of the few fishing trips where we didn't want to catch any more fish that day.

Thailand - Brian with 50 lb. catfish

13

LAKE MEAD, NEVADA

Bass

Lake Mead lies about 24 miles from Las Vegas, Nevada. The man-made lake was formed in 1935 when the Hoover Dam was built on the Colorado River. It is the largest reservoir in the USA servicing Nevada, Arizona, and California. The lake is over 100 miles long

My brother Clayton and his wife Bev were visiting us at our condo in Vegas when I convinced Clayton to try a half day of fishing on Lake Mead. He was in an adventurous mood, having already agreed to his first massage and a nighttime tour of the Vegas strip via helicopter.

I booked a trip and arranged the time and place to meet. We both needed fishing licenses, which sounded simpler than we expected. I think it took two stores and much hassle to finally get mine. Clayton got frustrated and didn't even bother getting one, until we got to the boat. There, our guide informed us he could issue one immediately. He could have told me that rather than saying I had to go to a store. His first trip will be his last trip with me.

As seems normal in fishing, the fish are not close to the launching spot. As we sped across the lake, Clayton used quite a few adjectives in describing the weather. It may get hot in Las Vegas, but that morning, the lake air was more than chilly. Fortunately, almost immediately Clayton caught a striped bass. We caught several more before returning to the dock. The guide cleaned the fish, and we were off to the condo. On the drive back Clayton told me he didn't like fishing because he never seemed to catch anything. He enjoyed the morning because he did.

I made and served soup and crackers for lunch. Clayton later told me that was the highlight of the day because it reminded him of growing up on the farm. Our collective catch provided more than one delicious feed.

OCEANS

1

HALIFAX NOVA SCOTIA, ATLANTIC OCEAN

Cod

As a boy, I often had to swallow a spoonful of horrid tasting cod liver oil. Cod liver oil is a source of Vitamin D that we prairie boys took in the winter to combat short days, which reduced sun exposure, a big source of Vitamin D. As an adult, I had an opportunity to fish for cod.

I attended a Chartered Accountants Convention in Halifax, Nova Scotia,. The cod fishing industry influenced many early settlements in the Maritime part of Atlantic Canada. After overfishing by Canadians and other European countries, the government stepped in and basically banned cod fishing in Canada in 1992.

It was not banned when I was in Halifax.

It didn't take me long to realize catching a cod was more a

nightmare than a dream. I boarded an old boat with several others. The weather was cold and damp, and the water was far from smooth. I was given a line with a baited hook and instructed to begin jigging.

Jigging is simply holding a baited line in the water and jerking your arm up and down like a piston with the bait at different depths in the water. I caught a cod and discovered they looked as bad as they had tasted.

Mission accomplished, but a valuable lesson learned. Don't do something just so you can say you did it.

2

HAMILTON, BERMUDA, ATLANTIC OCEAN

Bonefish

Bermuda is a British Island territory, famous for its pink sandy beaches. Located in the North Atlantic Ocean, it requires a three-hour flight from Edmonton to Toronto and another two-and a half-hour flight to Hamilton, Bermuda. We flew there to visit Wynne's daughter Laurie and her husband Paul. Laurie is a nurse, and he is a chartered accountant. They moved to Bermuda for job opportunities. We stayed at the Fairmont Southampton and enjoyed golfing on both courses on the island. I never thought fishing trips would be available.

That is until I recognized Bermuda is shaped like a fishhook and is an island surrounded by beautiful water. I soon found an advertisement to go fishing on a boat called "Jump dem Bones". I thought anyone with a boat name like that would be an interesting character. I was right. James Pearman owned the business and was our guide. He was the only person on the island to offer fly fishing. His goal was to make bone fishing in Bermuda a tourist attraction large enough to impact the economy. He charged about $500 US for a four-hour trip. He supplied the boat, the fly fish gear, and the expertise.

He picked us up at the hotel and a short time later we were on the water basking in the sun. The water was a beautiful blue and so clear, you could see the fish swimming. Unfortunately seeing the fish is not the same as catching them. You had to cast the fly behind the fish and reel the fly slowly across the water over the fish. Being a novice fishing with a fly reel, this proved a challenge for me. When I did cast successfully, the fish showed no interest.

After four hours of learning about our guide, his ambition, fly fishing and bonefish, I had not experienced so much as a bite. The weather was beautiful, the scenery spectacular, the company great and the catching non- existent. A true fisherman loves fishing, the catching is a bonus.

Fly fishing in Bermuda

3

ROCKPORT TEXAS, ATLANTIC OCEAN

Redfish

n September 2010, Allison informed me that her birthday present to me was a fishing trip to Rockport, Texas. To get to Rockport I had to first fly from Edmonton to Dallas, Texas, then Dallas to Waco. From there, it's a four-hour drive to Rockport. I was impressed that my daughter had learned I enjoy experiences as gifts much more than things.

It is a rare opportunity to spend time with your 'children' in such an environment. I got to see a large part of Texas on the road, spend a day on the water and an evening stay in a new city.

Rynhard led us out in an open-air motorboat under a blue sky, light jacket temperature, and a gentle breeze. Before a hook hit the water, Allison announced a competition for first fish, most fish, and biggest fish. Maybe I shouldn't have practiced playing Super Mario that summer when she was a young girl at the lake. I won our first game of Super Mario when she came home in the fall. She did not take losing lightly. I didn't have long to wait until she improved her game and once again could beat me. The competitive spirit was still alive and well.

A bonus experience was when the fire alarm went off at the motel in the middle of the night. I hadn't expected to get the excitement of getting up, going outside, and waiting to get back to my room.

I don't exactly remember who caught the most fish or the largest, but I will always remember Allison's smile when she landed the day's first redfish.

Allison caught the first redfish

Rynhard caught the largest redfish

Brian caught the most redfish

4

HAWAII, MEXICO, PACIFIC OCEAN

Marlin

I f you love to fish, you are likely to hear about the 1,800 lb. Pacific Blue Marlin caught in Hawaii in 1970. Hearing stories and seeing pictures of the beautiful blue marlin was enough for me to set a goal of catching one. For years, our family took an annual post-Christmas vacation to Hawaii. I booked many fish charters on those trips. I routinely caught Ahi, also called Yellowfin tuna, Mahi, also called Dorado and Ono, also called Wahoo.

I never caught a Blue Marlin.

My most memorable trip was taken one New Years' Day. My thinking was few people would be fishing with fewer guests on the boat. The odds of catching a marlin would be much improved. I could not have been more wrong. I didn't consider that the Captain might have a hangover and be functioning on little or no sleep. It quickly became obvious he had no interest or desire to catch a fish. He just put the boat on automatic cruise and went to lie down. Enjoy your boat ride on the ocean. I also went to sleep lying on the deck. I got so much sun on my face that my skin looked terrible. I wondered if my normal look would ever return. I would never have imagined how much damage you can get from too much sun.

For my next brilliant move, I rented a boat with no other people. If five people paid for a trip you would pick a number to determine your turn to catch the fish. If you drew number five you would not get a turn unless five fish were caught. The odds of getting a marlin were very small. Now I didn't have to wait to fish, it was always my turn.

My boat was beautiful, but it was not designed to be a fishing boat. The 'Captain' seemed more interested in serving tea from real china and telling me how great he was than whether I caught any fish. We spent the day washing hooks.

On one favourite day, Allison and her cousins Erin and RJ joined me for a day of fishing. It turned out they were not all immune from seasickness. "Chumming" is throwing food in the water to attract fish to your boat. Erin gave it a try. Next thing I knew, little Erin was in front of me yelling "What is so DAMNED funny?" Apparently laughing at someone throwing up is not funny to her. I asked the captain to take us back.

***

I once again came back to Canada without a marlin but with a new plan. I asked my assistant to call our travel agent to find the best place to catch marlin. The answer was Australia or Cabo San Lucas, Mexico. It is a seventeen-hour flight to Australia and only a three-and a half hour flight to Los Angeles and another couple hour flight to Cabo. So, I booked a Cabo fishing trip for Craig, Jim, Murray, and myself.

The biggest surprise of the trip was the flight's no-smoking section on Air Mexico. The last two rows were the only non-smoking seats. The air was just blue on that flight.

We checked into an old hotel on the harbour, within walking distance of our fishing boat.

Our boat was large enough for a crew of three and the four of us. We were excited about the possibilities this day might bring. Our enthusiasm waned as the day progressed. We covered a lot of water without any sign of a fish.

Late in the afternoon the motor roared, and we were off to a spot where several birds were circling above the water. Several other boats raced to the same location. Minutes later a few boats had 'hooked' up with a marlin and we were one of them.

Everyone had agreed I, as trip organizer, would get a shot at the first fish. It didn't take me long to realize fishing for marlin is work. I strapped on a belt to hold the rod and buckled up my seat belt. The fight was on! The boat was large enough my friends could sit up top and watch the battle. Marlins are huge, strong fish and it is no easy task reeling one in. It didn't help the water was rough and I was continually getting soaked as waves swept over the boat.

For the next 45 minutes I battled the fish and had it right up beside the boat, More than once the fish was right beside the boat and we got a video of it but couldn't land it. Suddenly, without warning, a crew member cut the line and the fish was gone. I couldn't believe it when he said, "Quitting time." I not only had not realized my dream but now was fourth in line to get another turn. Another turn never came since we never caught another marlin on that trip. Jim caught a large sailfish and Craig got his picture with it. I don't make a habit of having my picture taken with other peoples' fish.

Murray's highlight was playing 'birds in the bush' to determine who bought dinner. It is a simple game where you try to guess the number of coins each person has in their hand. Each player can have zero to three coins. Whoever guesses the correct number is eliminated and gets a free meal. You keep playing until only one remains. Craig didn't mind the first loss, but as the losses continued, his enjoyment waned. We had a great time and lots of excitement but still no marlin for me.

I booked another trip to Cabo. Craig and Jim returned and so did Clayton and Vern Poeter. We took the same flight and stayed in the same hotel. I knew having five people would increase my odds of landing a marlin. I fished with

Vern because he was more supportive of me landing a marlin. And I did!

Unfortunately, it was only 66 pounds which is very small for a marlin. I had realized my long-time dream, but it left me with an empty feeling. Still, it was large enough that I had my picture taken with it and had a taxidermist make me a replica. The second and last fish I had mounted.

The crew kept the fish but brought some to the hotel to prepare a meal for the lucky fishermen. That dinner proved to be quite an experience. Craig and Jim had wandered off and came back just before dinner. Clayton, Vern, and I had told them to prepare the fish and we warned them it was soon going to be served. But they decided to go for a shower. The meal arrived shortly after they left, and we ate while it was hot. When they returned for dinner we had finished, and they sat down for a meal of leftovers. But they did look sharp.

The legacy of my marlin was far from over. When it was delivered, I took it to the office and hung it on the boardroom wall. I once returned from a trip only to discover the bill was used to hang pretzels. Returning from a family vacation we discovered the marlin chained to the balcony over the family room. I then moved it to my office where it was given more respect. It remained in my office until David, Craig's son, spent a few weeks working with me. I noticed him eyeing the marlin and knew his mother would love it in her home. I asked him if he wanted it and he did. He is now married with children of his own and I know not the resting place of the marlin.

I returned to Cabo once more when Fred Helmer invited me to his condo for tuna fishing. I knew Cabo had a marlin tournament with a $1,000,000 first prize, but I didn't know of tuna tournaments. We weren't in a tournament, but we caught tuna and also had a line in trolling for marlin. Suddenly, I was handed the rod and strapped in the chair ready to reel in my second, much bigger marlin. Fred tightened the drag, just as the fish came flying out of the water and disappeared. The line had snapped as the drag was too tight. A good sturgeon and salmon guide is not necessarily a good marlin guide.

My quest to catch a marlin resulted in many days fishing, fun times with my brothers and friends, going to Hawaii and Mexico and the thrill of catching marlin. Sometimes pursuing a goal is more important than achieving it.

PESCA DEPORTIVA
CABO SAN LUCAS, MEXICO.
ANGLER BRIAN HESJE
FROM EDMONTON, CANADA
FISH STRIPED MARLIN
TACKLE 50 # TEST
TIME 35 MIN
WEIGHT 66 LBS
BOAT DORADO VI
CAPT RAMON/NOV-21-93

Brian finally caught a marlin.

5

WESTPORT, WASHINGTON, PACIFIC OCEAN

Albacore Tuna

Not long after seeing an ad for albacore tuna fishing in Westport I arranged a trip to catch one. Craig, Brent, Jim and I boarded a flight to Seattle where we rented a car and made the 2 ½ hour drive to Westport, Washington. Upon arrival we hit the local bar for some lunch. Westport only has a population of around 2000 so it's easy for locals to spot outsiders coming to fish. We were about to find out why they had knowing smiles on their faces when we told them we were going fishing.

We went shopping for groceries and I had to remind the lads we were only going to sea for two nights. We bought lots of groceries. The next day shortly after we left the dock, Craig asked the guide, "How far to the fishing area"? We were shocked when he said twenty-four hours.

No wonder the locals had been smiling.

Sit back and relax, we will be here for a while. Unfortunately, the ocean was far from being flat and my friends all came down with varying degrees of seasickness. The other two guests were a recently married couple. The bride stayed in her bunk the entire trip and appeared to not be enjoying the trip.

Albacore tuna travel in schools that can be as much as 19 miles wide. When a school is found, the fishing is amazing. The crew "chum" the water with live anchovies and every line in the water catches fish after fish. Best to enjoy because the next school might be found for a while. We each caught several fish, but the scenery was not spectacular. All you could see was water and waves.

After two nights on the boat, we were all happy to see land again. It seemed the memories of seasickness disappeared. The crew was ecstatic when we told them the fish and groceries were theirs to keep. Very few of our groceries had been eaten.

Albacore tuna could be stroked off the bucket list.

Brian with albacore tuna

6

LODGES, BRITISH COLUMBIA, PACIFIC OCEAN

Salmon

The memory of a Readers Digest article I read as a child about a man catching a coho salmon never left me. I was determined to catch one of these beautiful 'silver' fish and I have caught many over the years. But I didn't know the Pacific salmon family also included many species such as chinook, chum, sockeye and pink. I have now caught each type, but my focus soon was focused on the Pacific Chinook. They are the largest species of salmon and one weighing over thirty pounds is called a 'tyee'. Tyee means "the chief" in the coastal Indian language.

Campbell River is a city in British Columbia on the east coast of Vancouver Island. The city has boasted having the Tyee Club since 1924. To become a member of the club you must catch a chinook weighing 30 pounds or more and it must be done in a rowboat in a tyee pool. A guide once offered to row for me, and I never followed up. I have often regretted missing that opportunity.

I booked a trip to Campbell River for Keith and myself. We stayed in a lodge cabin with an elderly gentleman from California. He made it clear he was happy to enjoy the fresh air, the ocean, and the experience. The manager must have heard him because he got the worst guide. After day one with no fish, the guide was said to be a fine young man. After day two with no fish, he was the dumbest $#%$#% he had ever seen. Fishermen do lie.

I realized the thrill of catching my first salmon at Campbell River, but it was not as exciting as I had dreamed.

I went back to Campbell River on another trip paid for by my father-in-law. A memory was when one brother-in-law gave him a gift equal to the value of the trip. He did not want to feel he owed anyone. For some people accepting a gift is more difficult than giving one. I believe it is important to be able to do both.

We took two other trips on rented fishing boats. It's unbelievable that prairie boys with no knowledge of the sea could rent a large boat and play in the ocean. We always caught fish but never anything close to a tyee.

Brian Kirkpatrick, one of our store managers, and his son Cory picked me up in their truck late one afternoon. We drove from Edmonton all night, reaching Vancouver twelve hours later. A 90-minute ferry ride took us to Victoria and another two-hour drive up Vancouver Island got us to our destination of Parksville. We checked into a motel and Brian called his friend who owned the charter boat. The boat captain was a retired gentleman from the Prairies, but he knew where to fish. What made the trip special was canning the fish back at our motel. It never occurred to me that people would know how and want to can their own fish. While glad to have seen it, my plans were to have someone else can my fish.

The Queen Charlotte Islands were known as the best place to go if you wanted to catch big salmon. I fished there many times before 2012 when the British Columbia government changed the name to Haida Gwaii to honour the native heritage. I also fished there many times after the name changed. The first lodge I visited was called Peregrine Lodge. The lodge is named after the peregrine falcon.

The Peregrine Fishing Lodge officially opened on May 27, 1987. Previously the lodge had served as a lumber camp for Husby Forest Products which was owned by Dave Husby and situated in Naden Harbour in the Queen Charlotte Islands.

Initially it lodged guests of the logging company, but in 1989 they sold sport fishing trips, but only to those with private chartered flights. In 1991, they had their first year of private air charter trips from Vancouver to Masset. A helicopter then flew you from Masset to the lodge. It was also the year a record 270-pound halibut was caught. In

1992, the lodge hosted the first Fishing Derby, the first of many to follow. In 1994, Patrick Duffy, a star of the television show, "Dallas," hosted the first Ladies Fishing Derby. The next year, Geoff Courtnall of the Vancouver Canuck hockey team held his first derby. Participants included Wayne Gretzky, Frank Mahovlich, Bobby Hull, and other hockey greats. His tournaments raised over a million dollars for charity.

In 2001 new lodge buildings were completed and the previous lodge buildings became staff quarters. A new pitch and putt course replaced the driving range, where you hit floating golf balls into the ocean.

In 2010 Georgia Husby, Dave's wife, was named president of the Peregrine Fishing Lodge after his death. She is still operating the lodge in 2020.

Just as the lodge has a great history, I have a great history at the lodge. When I booked my first trip, I was confident my dream of catching a tyee would soon come true. The lodge gave a 'Tyee' pin to every lucky fisherman and I was determined to earn one. I would soon discover that catching a tyee is more difficult than imagined. I had many trips where I caught salmon weighing over twenty pounds. I even landed one that came in at 29, but none over 30. The manager kept telling me I should have been on the previous trip, or I should have taken the next trip. Lodges always have great fishing when you are not there.

You could book a three or four-day trip and I once

PRAIRIE FISHERMAN: FISHING MEMORIES

booked two trips to be on the 'trip before' and the 'trip after'. Neither resulted in me catching a tyee.

I eventually did land many a tyee at the lodge but the first came on my sixth trip. After all the close calls with the 28 and 29 pounders, many of which put up much bigger fights, this was a bit anticlimactic, but I was relieved. After I caught it, I immediately set my goal to catch a 40 or even 50-pounder. I achieved the forty-pounder at this lodge but not a 50 pounder. I took Rynhard on two trips to this lodge and his luck at landing a tyee is similar to mine.

***

Over the years, I competed in three tournaments that Peregrine Lodge hosted. When GPS became available, a new rule was implemented. You were not allowed to mark the spot where you caught a big fish. Some genius determined another big fish might come to the exact same spot. He forgot to tell the fish. It's interesting how paranoid some people are of someone else having any type of advantage.

My first tournament had simple rules. The person catching the biggest fish won first place. Each competitor paid an entrance fee for the trip cost and an additional $2,500 for prize money. They had 30 entrants, so the prize money totaled $75,000. The winner got $50,000, second got $15,000 and the third got $10,000. I went with Vern Burpee and we agreed to split the cash if either one of us won. Our odds of taking home a prize grew from one in thirty to one in fifteen.

I caught a salmon big enough to take fourth, just out of the money. Vern caught a fish that won second place. I was glad we had agreed to split the prize money, but he was less enthusiastic. He gave me $7,500 as agreed but it didn't feel like a win to me.

The second tournament was more complex. The winner was determined based on the weight of your two largest fish. This may seem like a good idea, but it didn't work out that way. Each night a draw was held to determine your guide for the next day. Guides are not all equal in skill or in integrity. Problems arose when the fishing was so slow nobody had caught two fish. This created the opportunity for people to cheat. Each boat had a fisherman and a guide.

If one person had landed one fish and his partner caught a fish, he could just swap lines and presto now one person had two fish. Of course, the guide was supposed to ensure this didn't happen. We became suspicious when one group offered us money to switch guides. I caught one fish weighing in the high twenties, which put me in the running to win if I landed a second one. I hooked another good-sized fish and could envision a triumph. My hopes faded quickly when a seal recognized my catch as a fish in distress and had it for a snack. Seals and sea lions often follow closely, let you do the work, and then dive in at the last minute and gobble up your catch before you can bring it in. I can still see that seal eating my victory. I will never know if a legitimate first prize was named, but I ended up going to other lodges.

Years later the manager called, saying they were hosting another tournament that might interest me. They were chartering a private plane to fly the competitors to the lodge. I called a friend, and we were registered. The flight took off from the private terminal in Vancouver. We were surprised to see so many people in their 20's and 30's on the trip. It was evident they had plenty of cash. They drove up in Cadillacs, wore nice clothes, and their conversations dealt with topics only people with money would have. We were explained the tournament rules which included being eighteen years of age. Everything appeared above board. It was a 'catch and release' tournament, so all fish caught would be released.

The first day went fine. Every two people were in a draw to determine the boat and guide they would have the next day. Every lodge has a couple of better boats and they have the best guides. This isn't a problem if the draw is done fairly. But on the second day, the same people got the best boats. When I questioned the manager, he said they had paid more for those boats. I couldn't believe that would ever occur in a tournament. Upon further questioning, he said they were members of the Hells Angels motorcycle gang. Now upset, I noticed many people fishing using red Islander fishing reels. They are known as the best and the most expensive salmon reels. They are made on Vancouver Island and the red reels are supposedly exclusively used by Hells Angels. Best to let sleeping dogs lie.

The best guides don't always result in the biggest catches. I caught a fish that weighed upwards of twenty pounds when weighed by the weighmaster before releasing it. I was now leading the tournament, but that wouldn't last. The eventual winner was the seven-year-old son of the leader of the other group. Rules had stated that you must be eighteen to enter the tournament. I took home third place money and a bear carving, but I vowed never to again enter a tournament there.

Years later, the manager, who I liked, called and convinced me to give the lodge another try. I booked a trip with my younger brother, Murray. Unfortunately, he called to say it wasn't going to work for him. I was having lunch with Rick Cormier. Rick was a longtime friend and now our company auditor. It surprised me when he said he would really like to go fishing.

The evening we arrived at the lodge I went to bed early to spend some time reading. I would often try to spend some time alone on a fishing trip. Rick was playing pitch and putt when I left. The next morning, he sarcastically said, "Thanks for leaving me with a bunch of people I didn't know." "But you meet people easily," I said. His reply was "I have to really work at it to have the courage to meet new people." This shocked me. I would never have thought that during the many years I had known him.

The fishing was good, and Rick loved it. He couldn't believe it when he asked me how long I had been doing this and I answered, "over thirty years." Last morning, I caught a 40-pounder but would have to release it to qualify for the largest fish, since I had already kept my legal limit of fish. The guide wanted Rick to claim it so we could keep it. We could have weighed and released it and qualified for the daily cash pool. Instead he told the fish master the fish belonged to Rick. I can still see the guide running out to the helicopter for his share of the winnings. The look on his face was priceless when I said Rick had told the truth and disqualified himself. Hopefully, the guide learned a lesson in integrity. I lost a tyee pin and recognition for releasing a big fish.

Rick vowed to do more fishing in the future. Sadly, he died of a heart attack while out running one morning that September, the same day as his processed fish was delivered to his home. While saddened to learn of his untimely passing I was grateful for the opportunity to introduce him to salmon fishing.

I didn't return to the lodge for years but wanted Rynhard, my son-in-law to catch his first tyee at the same lodge where I had caught mine. I had many more positive than negative memories at the lodge, so thought, "Why not try one more trip?" We enjoyed the time, but Rynhard did not catch a tyee, missing by one pound. Two years later we went back again.

This time the lodge owner was there with several of her relatives and friends. When she assigned our boat to one of her friends because the guide was having a lucky streak my patience with the lodge ended. I vowed never to go back and this time I never will.

I had many great memories over the years, but it is sad when the moral compass is not to be found.

In the late 1990's, our company began sponsoring fishing excursions.

We had a division that sold tires to the mining industry. We thanked some of our key customers by hosting a salmon fishing trip. I was in Vancouver to catch a flight to the Queen Charlotte Islands for my first business fishing trip.

I visited a friend the evening prior to departure. Some might consider Ted to be a bit eccentric, but I have always enjoyed his company. While rolling the lime gently on the counter to ensure perfection for his classic margarita, he shared his secret of how to catch a big fish. He said, "You simply steer the boat such that it makes a large circle. When the circle is complete you will see your fishing rod bend. You will have just caught a tyee."

I couldn't wait to test it.

The next morning, we took the two-hour flight to the Queen Charlotte Islands and were transported to the Hotei. The Hotei is a 115- foot yacht that was delivered to its owner, Jack Charles, in 1986. Jack Charles owned a large transport company called Arrow and Fountain Tire was their tire supplier. Jack's son captained the yacht for a few days of fishing.

The Hotei was a well-known boat often seen moored in the bay in Vancouver, B.C. during the 1986 Expo, hosting guests such as Lady Diana and Prince Charles. Other visitors included, Zsa Zsa Gabor, Mikhail Gorbachev, Boris Yeltsin, and many other recognizable personalities.

We ate and slept on the yacht but fished in groups of two on smaller boats that were anchored with us. I don't drive boats, so I had to fish with someone who did. Before the last day of fishing, the boys got drinking a bit and I noticed one guy never touched a drop. I started talking to him and he told me he didn't drink because he couldn't control it. I enjoyed our visit and was the first to head off to bed after we agreed to fish together the next day.

The next morning when I got up, my friend was asleep on the couch fully clothed. He was still sleeping after the others had left to fish. When he woke up, he sheepishly admitted he had broken his own rule and had a rough night. He did, however, agree to drive the boat so I could fish.

He didn't feel much like fishing.

We were having no luck and Danny, a salesman for Fountain Tire, who had the largest fish to date was heckling me from his boat. He had never fished for salmon and now he was beating an old 'pro.' This challenge required drastic action. Implementing Ted's tip, I instructed my driver to make a large circle in the ocean. Just as predicted, I caught a fish just as the circle was completed. Not only was it a fish, it was the largest salmon I had caught to date weighing 41 pounds.

After dinner, speeches, many laughs, and me receiving my Tyee certificate, a trophy, and the cash pool, I went out on the deck for some fresh air. Watching a beautiful sunset and breathing ocean air after a day fishing with good friends is as good as it gets.

I went on many fishing trips with this group. We fished at Lodges called Millbank, Englefield, and Hippa, but my fondest memory was at Salmon King Lodge, converted from an old cannery. The manager employed his two daughters and on one trip his son served as a guide. The son was dealing with some personal issues, but I readily agreed to go fishing with him. It was a good opportunity to try and help him gain some confidence. On the final morning of our trip he had no problem agreeing to take us fishing for a couple of hours. I caught two salmon that morning. One weighed 38 pounds but the other was 51 pounds. We had both caught our first fifty pounder, me as an angler, him as a guide.

The second twist of fate happened at an annual Fountain Tire convention. One year our theme was, "Roll On," a great slogan for tire dealers. Our team recruited Rick Hansen as our guest speaker, who delivered his inspirational message. When his team discovered that I like fishing, they invited me to his annual Rick Hansen Fishing Challenge at Langara Lodge in the Queen Charlotte Islands.

His foundation used the tournament to create awareness and raise funds for his Foundation. Each year, participants were asked to complete a pre-tournament questionnaire to familiarize you with the other guests.

One question was, "Who would you most like to be stranded on an isolated island with?"

I answered, "Jesus."

I was sitting in the boat with my arms folded, a habit of mine, when Fred Helmer, my guide came walking down to the pier. He later shared with me he was thinking, seeing me sitting there, that he was looking at a very boring three days. Instead, we became great fishing friends, going in the tournament for over a dozen years.

You can spend an entire day fishing without anything but hope. If you don't have patience you won't very likely like fishing. One day during the tournament we had been on the water for hours and I told Fred we could head back to the lodge if he was tired. He was not that kind of person and said we would be trying until closing time at six. It was shortly after five when he slipped our boat in front of another and my line started peeling off the reel. I don't know how far the fish ran, but when it tired, it was relatively easy to land. Once in the net I had caught a 53-pound salmon. We rushed to the dock and got it weighed before fishing closed for the day. My biggest salmon won me the first prize ATV, the cash pool, and the honour of being 'Mr. Bigfish".

The morning after catching the big fish, my rod had another big strike. I passed it to my fishing partner, our company CFO. It was his first-time fishing salmon but landed a 51-pound salmon. That catch won him, "Rookie of the Year." I wonder how I would have felt if he had landed a 54-pound salmon.

I have so many memories of this tournament. Rick and I have become very good friends and I even served on the Board of his Foundation. Fred and I have also become very good friends. The winning salmon Fred had mounted and proudly displayed on the wall of his tackle shop. Many times, we have also fished together for sturgeon.

The environment at Langara is almost surreal. Bald eagles are spotted every day, seals and sea lions are abundant and whale appearances are common. One day we witnessed the whales forming a circle around a large school of herring. They chased the herring to the surface and breach the water, eating hundreds of the little fish as they explode out of the water. It is awesome to see, but you have not experienced bad breath until you see this feat downwind.

Another day I asked Fred, "What would happen if a whale surfaces under a boat?" He said

"That never happens."

Shortly after we looked over and saw a whale surface under a 16 to 18-foot whaler boat, lifting the back out of the water. The moment was over quickly, and the boat didn't flip or anything. We rushed over to see if either one of the fishermen was hurt. They said no, but one guest requested they return to land so he could change clothes.

***

Anyone who thinks branding of a name is important would wonder why British Columbia would have West Coast Fishing Resort and West Coast Fishing Club, but they do. I fished with many of the West Coast Fishing Resort lodges many times but only one at the 'Club.' An interesting trip occurred at the Resort Milligan Lodge. I went on a trip with the owners of a company that I sat as a board member. I fished with Warren every day and he caught four tyee fish. I caught none sitting right next to him.

The Club is very close to the Langara Lodge and it is like a five-star hotel. Rynhard joined me there for two trips. One day we each caught a tyee salmon. He didn't find it funny when I pointed out we had each caught a tyee but only I had landed one. Catching a tyee is still on his bucket list.

This lodge has a trip where they bring in celebrity chefs and offer a cooking and fishing experience. Wynne and I invited a tire dealer from the USA and his wife to attend. His wife, not him, liked to fish. First day he caught and released a 44-pound salmon and the second day Wynne caught and released a thirty plus tyee. Fishing doesn't necessarily reward just those that love to fish.

Another memorable trip was to Duncanby Lodge at Rivers Inlet, B. C. with my older brother Morris. This was a 'fund-raising' trip for a salmon hatchery and Rick Hansen was there to give his support. Morris got to meet Rick and fished with him one day. He also got to catch a salmon.

The trip that I will never forget was on September 11, 2001. I remember where I was that morning. Craig, Jim, Vern, and I flew into Vancouver early in the morning and took a limo to the nearby terminal to catch our plane to the lodge. We were going to make this a memorable trip. While checking in, I glanced up at a television and saw an airplane fly into the World Trade Tower. I knew we would be going nowhere that day. We were lucky to book a hotel room before many knew what was happening.

It was a surreal day, watching the news all day in complete disbelief. It is ironic that I was off to do something I loved, the day the world changed forever in a very negative way.

After three days, we were bussed to Vancouver Island and were taken by boat to the lodge. We were supposed to get a week fishing but only got a few days. When we asked the manager about a partial refund for the days we didn't use, he said, "It wasn't his fault". It wasn't ours either, but we let it go. Never take for granted the days we have to do the things we love.

I may have spent more hours fishing for salmon and caught more salmon than goldeye, but had it not been for goldeye I would not likely ever have caught a salmon.

Brian , Fred, and Rick with winning fish

RICK HANSEN
FISHING CHALLENGE

Brian Congrats on the Big Fish! Many thanks! Rick

Langara Fishing Challenge competitors

Mr. Big Fish celebration

Brian receiving trophy from Mike Reid

Many whales provided spectacular sights.

Wynne with her tyee

Brian and Rynhard with day's catch

A few of Brian's tyee pins

Rynhard with his 29 pound salmon. Tyee is still on bucket list

CONCLUSION

As a boy I spent many hours thinking about what I'd like to accomplish in my future. As a senior I spend many hours thinking about my accomplishments. I can remember many things that I wish I had not done. I can remember many more that I am glad that I have done. I cannot remember a single day fishing that I regret.

If you enjoy something my advice to you is to MAKE time to do it. If you don't you will more likely think of regrets than of positive memories.

ABOUT THE AUTHOR

You can throw a stone from the back door of Brian's childhood home on the farm and have it land in the South Saskatchewan River. He spent many hours at the river fishing for goldeye with a 'throw line' and with grasshoppers as bait. In his mind he was fishing for food for the family. In his brothers minds he was fishing to get out of work.

Years later he mentioned how much he loved fishing to his poker playing friends and one asked him when was the last time you went on a planned fishing trip? It had been years. It was that night he decided not a year would pass without having at least one planned fishing trip. A promise he has kept for decades.